YOUR KNOWLEDGE HAS VALUE

AF137099

- We will publish your bachelor's and
  master's thesis, essays and papers

- Your own eBook and book -
  sold worldwide in all relevant shops

- Earn money with each sale

Upload your text at www.GRIN.com
and publish for free

Bibliographic information published by the German National Library:

The German National Library lists this publication in the National Bibliography; detailed bibliographic data are available on the Internet at http://dnb.dnb.de .

Imprint:

Copyright © 2019 GRIN Verlag
Print and binding: Books on Demand GmbH, Norderstedt Germany
ISBN: 9783346038821

This book at GRIN:

https://www.grin.com/document/497717

Thomas Mayer

Eye Gaze Interaction for a Mobile Text Application. A New Interface Concept

GRIN Verlag

GRIN - Your knowledge has value

Since its foundation in 1998, GRIN has specialized in publishing academic texts by students, college teachers and other academics as e-book and printed book. The website www.grin.com is an ideal platform for presenting term papers, final papers, scientific essays, dissertations and specialist books.

Visit us on the internet:

http://www.grin.com/

http://www.facebook.com/grincom

http://www.twitter.com/grin_com

LUDWIG-MAXIMILIANS-UNIVERSITÄT MÜNCHEN
Department "Institut für Informatik"

Bachelorarbeit

Eye Gaze Interaction for a Mobile Text Application

Thomas Mayer

Bearbeitungszeitraum: 05.11.2018 bis 25.03.2019

Zusammenfassung

Ein übliches Element einer Benutzeroberfläche zum Auslösen einer Aktion ist der Button, der traditionell berührt oder angeklickt wird. Ein neues Konzept wird eingeführt, das die Standardfunktionalität eines Buttons um blickbasierte Funktionen erweitert, der GazeButton. Er fungiert als universelle Schnittstelle für blickbasierte UI-Interaktionen während einer klassischen Berührungsinteraktion. Er ist einfach mit bestehenden Benutzeroberflächen zu kombinieren und ergänzt sie unaufdringlich, da er den Benutzern die Freiheit lässt, zwischen klassischer und blickbasierter Interaktion zu wählen. Außerdem ist er unkompliziert, weil alle neuen Funktionen lokal an ihn gebunden sind, und obwohl er nur ein kleines UI-Element ist, ist er aufgrund seiner Blickkomponente für Interaktionen im gesamten Display und darüber hinaus verwendbar. Der GazeButton wird anhand einer Textbearbeitungsanwendung auf einem Multitouch-Tablet-PC demonstriert. So kann beispielsweise ein Wort ausgewählt werden, indem man es ansieht und auf den GazeButton tippt, wodurch anstrengende körperliche Bewegung vermieden wird. Für solche Beispiele werden konkrete systematische Entwürfe vorgestellt, die visuelle und manuelle Benutzereingaben kombinieren, woraufhin die blickbasierte mit der berührungsbasierten Textauswahl in einer Benutzerstudie verglichen wird.

Abstract

A common element of a user interface for initiating an action is the button that is traditionally touched or clicked. A new concept is introduced that extends the standard functionality of a button with advanced gaze-based functions, the GazeButton. It acts as an universal interface for gaze-based UI interactions during a classic touch interaction. It is easy to join with existing UIs and unobtrusively complementary because it keeps the users' freedom to choose between classic and gaze-based interaction. In addition it is uncomplicated, because all new functions are locally bound to it, and, despite being just a small UI-Element, it is usable for interactions throughout the display and even beyond because of its gaze component. The GazeButton is demonstrated using a text editing application on a multitouch tablet computer. For example, a word can be selected by looking at it and tapping the GazeButton avoiding strenuous physical movement. For such examples, concrete systematic designs are presented that combine visual and manual user input whereafter the gaze based text selection is compared with the classic touch based one in a user study.

Aufgabenstellung

Typing on wide touch screens takes longer time than attaching a normal keyboard to it. Recently, the use of gaze as an interaction modality became ubiquitous. It is now enabled in public displays, laptops and soon in mobile phones. By the use of gaze, we can enhance the typing experience by combining touch with gaze interaction. Accordingly, in this thesis, we aim to enhance text entry on wide touch screens with the use of gaze.

Tasks:

- Review state of the art of using gaze and touch as interaction modality.

- Implementation of touch and gaze enhanced methods.

- Carry out a lab study to evaluate the method usability.

- Analyze and report the results.

Contents

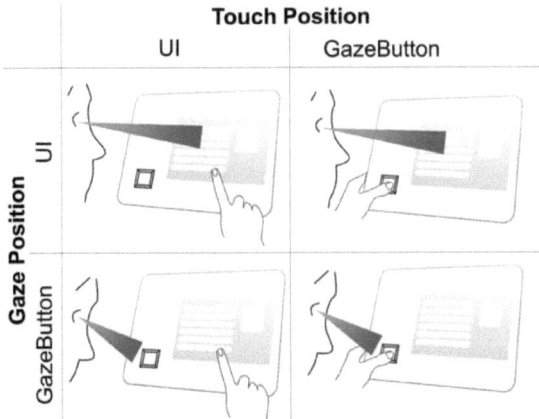

Figure 1.1: The GazeButton: An augmented button that expands the standard UI interaction (top left) with three new input modalities that, identified by eye tracking, can be used for interaction.

1 Introduction

The dominant computer interface is based on a 2D GUI ever since the introduction of the direct manipulation interface by Shneiderman [29]. Tablet users usually use the index finger or thumb for interaction, whereby interaction with the fingers often makes large parts of the screen useless by obscuring them during the interaction. This basic interaction is usually made possible by a common GUI element called the 'button' whose functionality stayed the same, whether on a desktop PC, smartphone or tablet PC. The user selects the button by hand, either indirectly with the mouse, or directly on a touch screen and thus causes an action. This thesis examines how this basic button concept and the UI interaction can be extended and improved by using gaze recognition.

Due to advances in the technology behind eye tracking it is now possible to integrate complete eye trackers into the screen or use them as external devices on existing displays [13] [33]. Research has investigated numerous interaction methods and device types [30] [12] [8] [19] [31] [46], including hands-free interaction on smart watches through smooth pursuit eye movements [8], moving an object by looking at it followed by a button press and mouse movement where the mouse acts as a relative positioning device [12], and several types of eye typing [19]. These methods were explored in isolation as general selection methods or as alternatives to standard manual input methods. Recently, the combination of gaze and touch for interaction with large displays using various techniques on mobile devices has been attempted [36]. It is not completely clear, however, how gaze and manual input can be reconciled, nor how gaze recognition can harmonize with established UI concepts, especially when applied to tablet computers.

Creating the GazeButton an innovative UI element has been built extending the conventional button concept by adding semantic usage of the user's eye movement to it. The underlying concept is to use the additional gaze data and its possible combinations with touch interaction to make a single button much more expressive simplifying the multiple manual interactions by taking into account the user's gaze during manual input [23]. This UI design has several advantages.

By combining the two input methods gaze and touch that can easily and naturally be used at the same time there can be a larger number of different interactions without needing additional UI space when compared to a conventional button.

Also, because of the little space that is needed by a single relatively small UI Element, the GazeButton can easily be integrated into existing UIs and still does not interfere with interactions that are already there. The UI remains intact with all its previous functionality.

Furthermore, despite the small size of the GazeButton it can be used for interactions on the whole screen since gaze can easily reach throughout the screen without needing additional UI space nor obscuring existing one.

As figure 1.1 illustrates, the GazeButton allows for three new input states that can be used for user interaction in addition to the conventional interaction (top left). The new states are:

1. Gaze UI - Touch GazeButton (top right)   The user looks at the UI while they press the GazeButton. For example the user looks at a text field and taps the button to place the cursor at gaze position but if the user looks at another button the GazeButton might be linked to that button and act just like the button that is gazed at so that the user does not have to move the whole arm to the other button which would obscure the screen.

2. Gaze GazeButton - Touch UI (bottom left)   In this case the GazeButton can be looked at to modify a classic UI touch function for instance to enter a shift character instead of a lower-case one when the letter is touched on an on-screen keyboard while looking at the GazeButton. As well as **1.** (top right) this state can be used to add functionality at any point in the screen with just one unimposing button.

3. Gaze GazeButton - Touch GazeButton (bottom right)   Both looking at and touching the GazeButton forms another unambiguous interaction which can be used to trigger an action.

In this thesis those possibilities will be explored on implemented examples in a text editing application prototype on a touchscreen tablet computer. Subsequently, a user study that has been designed and conducted to evaluate one of the GazeButton's new interaction techniques is presented and evaluated. Among other findings, the study showed that, at a specific font size, participants preferred the new gaze based text selection over the conventional touch based one.

2   Related Work

This section discusses related work that involves research in the design of UIs for handheld devices as well as research in eye-tracking based interaction.

2.1   UI for Handheld Devices

There are some different challenges on mobile devices as opposed to desktop computers so researchers focused on the handheld touchscreen UI to improve it and make it more ergonomic to use. For example there is the grip and reach issue, meaning that the necessity to hold the device in at least one hand restricts the interaction possibilities of the holding hand. This issue with regard to thumb reachability has been investigated extensively by Bergstrom-Lehtovirta and Oulasvirta by modeling the "functional area of the thumb" of the holding hand [2], by Trudeau et al. with a special focus on thumb typing with both hands on different on-screen keyboards on tablet computers [34], by Wolf and Henze in terms of pointing techniques on two-handed tablet interactions [43], by Odell and Chandrasekaran who focused on tablet computer thumb interaction [22] and by Wolf et al. who tried to better understand the target selection on tablets by taking into account the hand's kinematic model [44].

In addition various methods were suggested to avoid the grip and reach issue, in some cases allowing unimanual tablet interaction. Cheng et al., for instance, developed a prototype that uses grip sensing to adapt the on-screen keyboard to the current hand positions of the user [5] and Wagner et al. pointed out that UI elements can be moved automatically to the reachable area of the holding hand [40] while Hinckley et al. illustrated how pre-touch sensing, that detects multiple fingers above and around the screen, can be used to adapt the UI to the user's holding position by estimating the finger and grip posture before they interact with the screen [9]. As for gaze-based solutions, Pfeuffer and Gellersen suggested to combine gaze and touch interaction to enable users to reach the whole screen using relaxed thumb touches that refer to the user's gaze position [25]. A difficulty for users in their approach is that there is no visible UI element bound to this interaction.

In another work without eye-tracking, Pfeuffer et al. presented "thumb buttons" that are used to manipulate and extend the functionality of a stylus in an indirect way [26]. Those thumb buttons were placed near the anticipated position of the user's grasp.

In this thesis the GazeButton is used similar to these thumb buttons but with a new gaze modality and without a stylus. Through the GazeButton the users are presented with a dedicated visual element for the oftentimes unfamiliar gaze interaction, making it more obvious and easier to understand.

2.2   General Gaze Interaction

In the works of Bolt [3] early research on eye tracking technologies and the progress made in it can be found. From those works one can learn about the beginning of gaze based interactions, the beginning of using eye tracking to give control to the users instead of merely observing the users' viewing direction with it, which has been done before that. The idea was to use gaze interaction to give users the possibility not to be overwhelmed by many moving images at the same time ("World of Windows"[3]) in a stimulus-flooded world, "making the eye an output device"[3]. He saw high potential for gaze based interactions in the future with regard to interactive graphics. Such graphics became extremely common and diverse to this day. The usefulnus of eye movements also has been studied about 9 years later by Jacob [12] who pointed out that the barrier to using eye movement as a medium does not lie in the eye tracking technology. Instead, he saw the need to explore interaction techniques that enable users to perform gaze based human-computer interaction in a natural, unintrusive way. For example, using the eye blink for a signal has been rejected for being unnatural and requiring distracting deliberate thinking. With this naturalness in mind, Jacob implemented gaze based interaction techniques and alternatives of them like:

Scrolling Text   by looking at arrows appearing above the first and below the last line of text where the text only scrolls if there is more text in the corresponding direction that can not be displayed within the visible area. The text then always scrolls when the user is looking at one of the described arrows. Unwanted scrolling is excluded based on the assumption that the user will look at the moving text when it starts scrolling which then stops the scrolling because the gaze moves away from the just viewed arrow.

Selecting an Object   by looking at it and pressing a key or by looking at it for a predetermined amount of time (dwell time) that can be very short if a wrong selection can be undone by a new selection following it. Jacob thought the dwell time approach to be "much more convenient"[12], leading to "excellent results"[12] with 150-250 ms dwell time. As a good use for this method a display with two areas is proposed where one area contains several objects while the other area acts as a "continous attribute display"[12] always showing information about the last viewed object.

Moving an Object   by selecting it like already mentioned, followed by a button press and moving the mouse where the mouse movement between the press and release of the button is translated into object movement or by selecting *and* moving the object with the eyes whereby a button is pressed to indicate the start of the movement and released to indicate the end of the movement. In the latter technique, instead of moving the object fluidly it actually jumps suddenly to the new eye fixation after about every 100 ms and stays there without motion to avoid unwanted motion caused by "eye jitter" [12] which is small movements of the eye that Jacob found to be normal in humans, usually rotating the eye less than one degree. Despite the hypothesis that this translation of eye movement into object movement would be hard to use, moving the object with ones eyes turned out to be more convenient making the mouse movement in the alternative technique feel redundant and unnatural.

A similar way of selecting objects with the eye without dwell time by button press and moving an object by linking eye movement to object movement on the screen is going to be presented in this thesis, using the GazeButton for text selection.

Later, in 1999, Zhai et al. [46] explored the use of eye gaze as an input medium as well and illustrated three reasons for using gaze interaction, especially for gaze pointing, namely:

- Making pointing possible for users who can not use their hands because of physical handicap or having their hands occupied with other tasks

- Accelerating interaction, taking advantage of the relatively high movement speed of eyes in comparison to other body parts

- Reducing physical stress and fatigue caused by typical computer interaction devices like mouse and keyboard by reducing or replacing their use with eye interaction which needs less energy.

In the same paper [46] Zhai et al. clarified two problems they thought previous gaze pointing techniques suffer from, one being that the subconsious motions of the eye, called "eye jitter" by Jacob [12], lead to a precision with a target area whose diameter is bigger than the size of a typical scrollbar and much bigger than the size of a typical character in a typical screen setup, the other being the fact that using dwell time to initiate actions is unnatural as the eyes are often used for tasks like searching without the intention of initiating an action which leads to unwanted dwell time actions when looking at an object for too long in a usual search. This problem of unwanted dwell time actions is called "'Midas touch' problem"[12] by Jacob.

With those two mentioned problems of other gaze pointing techniques as a basis Zhai et al. stated that "it is unnatural to overload a perceptual channel such as vision with a motor control task"[46] so they wanted to improve traditional gaze pointing with their own approach called "MAGIC (Manual And Gaze Input Cascaded)"[46] with the aim to keep pointing and selection primarily manual using gaze just as a secondary aid which is achieved by a combination of gaze based and manual pointing that highly reduces manual cursor movement by letting the cursor jump to an eye gaze area around the target, followed by manual cursor movement for fine pointing and clicking for selection.

In the following year Sibert and Jacob evaluated their eye gaze interaction techniques [30], discovering that their gaze based object selection (already described in this thesis) was faster than common mouse selection proving the speed advantage of the eyes over the more physically demanding alternative.

In 2012, Stellmach and Dachselt [31] again pointed out some solutions for the lower precision of gaze selection in contrast to mouse selection such as using bigger GUIs and combining gaze and manual input like in Zhai et al.'s "MAGIC" interactions. They tested those solutions and found them outperforming gaze-only cursor selection and being highly adaptable to handheld devices.

2.3   Gaze Interaction on handheld devices

Not being confined to desktop computers the use of gaze based interaction techniques has found use with powerful handheld devices as well and in 2007, Drewes et al. [7] tested the feasibility of gazed based interaction techniques for mobile phones in a user study even before phones had the needed processing power for eye tracking technology. They found that gaze interaction is attractive for mobile phone users. Recently, in 2018, Khamis et al. [13] presented a complete view on the past, present and future of eye tracking on handheld devices and described arisen challenges and opportunities in this area that suggest further research. Khamis et al. referred to the three tenses in the history of eye tracking as follows:

Past   A phase beginning in the early 2000s, when eye tracking on mobile devices was new and handheld consumer devices lacked the necessary processing power for eye tracking which was assumed to change in the future.

Present   The current time, after experiencing past advances in built-in front-facing cameras and processors of mobile devices, making it increasingly practical to investigate gaze interaction that involves eye tracking on unmodified handheld devices.

Future   A phase where eye tracking is used widely and seamlessly as part of manifold daily interactions.

Khamis et al. described the past and present of handheld eye tracking considering "gaze behaviour analysis"[13], "implicit gaze interaction"[13], "explicit gaze interaction"[13] and the "lessons learned"[13] in that phase while discussing opportunities and challenges when it comes to the future phase.

In the past, the front-facing cameras of mobile devices were usually not sufficient for real-time eye tracking. As a result, the initial research involving eye tracking on mobile devices used external eye trackers like head-mounted devices or remote commercial eye trackers or they even expanded handheld devices by building their own hardware. This commitment testifies to high motivation in researching this topic and high believe in the advancement of eye tracking technology in this early phase in the history of mobile gaze interaction that nevertheless lead to insights like the finding that gaze bahaviour when scanning through search results differs on large screens in comparison to small screens [15] as they are common in mobile devices. As early as 2005, Dickie et al. [6] presented a system called "eyeLook" that is able to recognize whether a user is looking at a mobile device or not, creating the possiblity to pause moving content on the screen such as a running video automatically when the user is not looking at it. Khamis et al. [13] stated that, despite problems with ecological validity in the past research in mobile gaze interaction, there would be a clear message that using eye bahaviour such as gestures and smooth pursuit is more promising, better perceived and less reliant on calibration than dwell time based solutions which makes solutions without dwell time seem more suitable for handheld devices.

Khami et al.'s [13] present phase started with gaze interaction research on unmodified handheld devices that increased drastically since 2010. In that year, Bulling and Gellersen [4] discussed the aspects of upcoming research on eye tracking on handheld devices, stating that appliactions for gaze based interaction are typically limited to stationary setups but also mentioning the first video-based eye tracker that fits almost completely inside an ordinary glasses frame (Tobii Glasses).

On unmodified gaze-enabled handheld devices it became possible to do research in this field with high ecological validity. For example, Miluzzo [21] proposed "EyePhone", a system that uses the front camera of a mobile phone and machine learning algorithms to detect the position on the phone display the user is looking at and in 2012, Vaitukaitis and Bulling [39] were able to detect gaze gestures with an accuracy of 60 % with a prototype that runs entirely on an unmodified android smartphone. In the same year, Stellmach and Dachselt [31] explored through a user study how gaze as an interaction technique can be used with handheld devices to highlight important information on a distant larger screen while searching through images. For this they extended Zhai et al.'s MAGIC pointing [46] and adapted it to touch input using touch interaction for fine selection and developed two new variations called "MAGIC touch" [31] and "MAGIC tab" [31] that allowed users to fine position the cursor with touch input and iterate through a list of objects that are spatially close to the user's viewpoint. Stellmach and Dachselt's aim was in particular to figure out how enjoyable their gaze supported selection techniques appeared to the users finding out that their MAGIC variations were very robust concerning inaccurate gaze data and thus leading to low eye strain, high performance and high reported usability. Especially in their "MAGIC tab" they saw high potential for future works for allowing fast and accurate selection of small targets that are close together or overlapping.

From 2011, Turner et al. combined gaze and touch to extend the user's physical reach across devices giving them the power to interact with remote displays [38] [37] [36]. This multimodal UI has been particularly explored on tablet and desktop computer touchscreens by Pfeuffer et al. [23] [24], demonstrating a high potential of gaze interaction when it comes to providing benefits by extending the usual touch input. For example, they gave users freedom in their choosing of the area on the screen they use for touch interaction by translating finger taps and multi touch gestures on the screen to the point the user is looking at instead of using the touch points as point of action [23]. This not only lets users choose freely where on the screen they touch without changing the action to be performed but also avoids occlusion of important areas on the screen by the users' arms or hands because users would touch the screen somewhere where they do not obscure important information if they are presented this possibility.

In 2015, Mariakakis et al. [20] introduced "SwitchBack", a system that, like "EyePhone"[21], uses the front facing camera of a smartphone, in this case for enabling the phone to detect when the user starts or stops focusing their visual attention on the phone using Mariakakis et al.'s algorithm "Focus and Saccade Tracking" (FAST) [20] that additionally was able to identify how many lines of text a user has read in a controlled study with a mean absolute error of 3.9 %. This ability has been used to highlight the last read line of the user after a distraction occured in a smartphone text reading scenario with distractions improving the average reading speed by 7.7 %.

Such eye tracking techniques that only need a front-facing camera and software to compute the user's gaze coordinates based on the iris positions in the camera's captured image belong to the field of *computer vision based gaze tracking* which Hohlfeld et al. described as "promising low-cost realization of gaze tracking on mobile devices" [10] as the built-in hardware of smartphones is sufficient so no cost-intensive extra hardware is needed and it can be improved by new algorithms.

To find out how applicable computer vision based gaze tracking on mobile devices is in practice, Hohlfeld et al. [10] started researching this topic based on two user studies using an unmodified Nexus 7 (2013) tablet and Wood and Bulling's "EyeTab" algorithm for binocular gaze estimation [45] which is open source and was able to achieve a gaze estimation accuracy of 6.88° of visual angle at near-realtime speed of 12 frames per second [45]. Hohlfeld et al.'s first user study on computer vision based gaze tracking [10] focussed on assessing aspects they saw as crucial to the use of mobile gaze tracking such as the effects of varying conditions like viewing distance and lighting, including the use of glasses. They found out that different lighting and viewing distances can have a large effect while the use of glasses of the person whose eyes are tracked barely affects eye tracking performance. Problems they identified were the limited accuracy of EyeTab in their use case and that the eye tracking accuracy changes from the top to the bottom of the screen with the point on the screen the user is looking at when the front-facing camera is built-in at the bottom.

With this limitations in mind, Hohlfeld et al. conducted a second user study [10] finding out that in their setup it is possible to recognise users' word fixations with a recognition rate of up to 77% in the top row on the screen but also that this recognition rate decreases down to 8% in the bottom row on the screen where the angle between the gaze of the user and the camera is very low so they suggested to only use this technique for detecting word fixations when the tested words are located in the upper half of the screen, relatively far away from the camera.

After stating that gaze based interaction using front-facing cameras of mobile consumer devices is expected to improve and in fact opens great opportunities like novel usability testing outside labs but also that there still are improvements needed, Khamis et al. [13] described those oportunities and challenges in their future phase of gaze-enabled handheld mobile devices, pointing out that, while in the early days of eye tracking the challenges mainly related to hardware, nowadays many problems can be solved with software, nevertheless attributing high importance to "front-facing *depth* cameras" [13] believing that this new hardware will catalyse mobile eye tracking, making it widely used by consumers in everyday life.

This thesis takes inspiration from the described observations that confirm the attractiveness of gaze based interaction on handheld devices, and works to increase the experience in such interactions in the context of a text editing application on a touch screen tablet computer.

2.4   Eye Typing

Eye typing is the entering of text by utilizing the recognition of the user's gaze, which in case of pure eye typing enables even people to type who can only move their eyes, so the first gaze typing that was introduced in the 1970s is an application for disabled people [19]. Since then, much research has been done in this area trying to increase the speed and accuracy of eye typing.

2.4.1   Dwell Time Based Eye Typing

Despite the Midas touch problem [12] inherent in dwell time based approaches, it is the only way of eye typing for some disabled people and there are many dwell time based eye typing methods. One of them is "pEyeWrite" [11] which uses two pie menus containing characters for typing. Those menus resulted from the desire to unify interfaces for gaze control. The initial bigger pie menu contains five characters per slice in six slices. If the user looks at one slice for 400ms they select it and a second, smaller pie menu appears that partly overlaps the bigger pie menu, mainly where the selected big slice is located. The smaller pie menu contains only one character per slice in its five slices which contain every character of the selected slice of the bigger pie menu. The user then selects a slice of the smaller pie menu by looking at it for 400ms and thus enters the character of the selected slice. Novice users achieved a maximum typing speed of 13.45 wpm with pEyeWrite and an average speed of 7.85 wpm. Another dwell time based eye typing method is "GazeTheKey" [28], which arised from the idea of making eye typing keys more dynamic, embedding word predictions into them and using a "two-step dwell time" [28].

2.4.2   Dwell Time Free Eye Typing

Without dwell time it is possible to type faster as there is no waiting involed and the Midas touch problem is avoided. One of the fastest eye typing applications until this day is "Dasher" with which 12 participants in a longitudinal user study, conducted by Tuisku et al. in 2008 [35], achieved an average eye typing speed of 2.49 wpm in the first and 17.26 wpm in the tenth session, one participant achieving 23.11 wpm average speed in session 9. Ward and MacKay, inventor and developer of Dasher [42], stated that after an hour of practice with Dasher users could write up to 25 wpm compared to 15 wpm on an on-screen keyboard. Furthermore, on-screen keyboard users were not only much slower but also had a fivefold as high error rate compared to Dasher users. Dasher is dwell time free, using pointing gestures in a dynamically changing graphical display of letters [41].

Another dwell time free eye typing application is "EyeSwipe" by Kurauchi et al. [17] which scans gaze paths to enter whole words at once that are selected out of a set of word suggestions after only the start and end of the swipe path are selected explicitly. To enable explicit eye selection without dwell time, Kurauchi et al. developed the selection mechanism "reverse crossing" [17] that works by 1) looking at the key that should be selected, 2) looking at the selection button that appears above the key and 3) looking back to the key that should be selected which then results in selecting it.

2.4.3   Eye Typing in Security and VR

Eye-typing also has been used in the security area. For example, Kumar et al. developed "Eye-Password" [16], a method for gaze based PIN and password entry that prevents shoulder-surfing, is only slightly slower than using a keyboard and is preferred over traditional methods by test subjects [16]. Khamis et al. designed a similar method called "GazeTouchPIN" [14] that combines gaze and touch to enter a PIN on the phone. Such methods make it hard for attackers to spy the password because gaze input is invisible unless you observe the eyes of the user.

Even in the context of virtual reality, eye typing has been explored. Recently, Rajanna and Hansen investigated eye typing in VR through two user studies with 32 people [27] using a VR headset with an eye tracking unit. They used dwell time based eye typing as well as eye typing with gaze selection and manual clicking for confirmation, both with a 2D keyboard that fits inside the user's view and with a 3D curved keyboard that is larger than the user's view, requiring head movement to be able to see and select all keys. Furthermore, the users executed the typing tasks while sitting as well as while biking. Results inlcude that, with the simple gaze typing methods Rajanna et al. implemented, gaze typing in VR is practical but confined, that the large curved keyboard increased physical strain and reduced typing speed in comparison with the smaller 2D keyboard and that, with a dwell time of 550 ms, participants performed better with the gaze and click solution and tended to prefer the method with clicking over the dwell time based one.

The previously described applications of gaze interaction focussed on several input methods or specific application cases. A different perspective is presented in this thesis, focussing on the extension of touch typing by using gaze interaction while keeping the freedom of typing conventionally, without losing the new functionality.

3   Gaze enhanced Text Editing

This section explains the prototype application for gaze enhanced text editing that has been developed for this thesis.

3.1   Explanation of important Components

For easier understanding, in the following, some components of the application prototype that are also illustrated in figure 3.1 are explained beforehand. There are three main interaction areas in the software that are important to the system to decide which action should be performed after an interaction in those areas:

Text Area This is the area on the screen where all text is displayed for direct manipulation, always containing a blinking cursor or a green marked area, indicating the current position for manipulating the text or the current selection of the text. The text area stretches from a bit under the middle of the screen to the top of the screen, including all of its width.

Keyboard The keyboard is another 2D area on the screen that contains all the keys of the on-screen keyboard of the application and is used for all the text manipulation. It takes up the remaining room on the screen that is not covered by the text area.

GazeButton The GazeButton is actually a part of the keyboard, belonging to the same class as all the other keys but it plays a special role in terms of interaction, both concerning touch and gaze, which justifies the treatment as an area of its own. It is located both in the bottom left and in in the bottom right of the screen where both instances inherit the same functions. In practice, one of those instances might suffice.

Figure 3.1: A screenshot of the running text editing application with markings indicating the text area (orange rectangle), the keyboard (green rectangle), both instances of the GazeButton (red rectangles) and the green text cursor (within the yellow ellipse).

3.2 Design Considerations

Other than works that aimed to design interfaces for two-thumb text entry on tablet computers [34] [2], this thesis aims to provide more functionality in text based applications by using gaze recognition while keeping the UI straightforward. Through simplification, the mental and physical stress during tablet usage is reduced, especially regarding arm effort when using gaze instead of large arm movement. The newly presented GazeButton can be used in several ways to improve the user experience. Trying to retain simplicity and coming up with intuitive interaction techniques, the following points can be taken into consideration:

Where the user looks The user's gaze is sensed by the eye tracker and then translated into 2D coordinates to detect where the user looks on or beside the screen as the gaze is not limited by screen dimensions. Since the user usually looks at the screen, the gaze coordinates are specified in a coordinate system whose origin is at a corner of the screen and all the gaze points correspond to pixels on the screen or imaginary pixels next to the screen with the same point density. In the text editing application of this thesis, these gaze points outside of the screen are used to expand selection ranges of objects near the screen borders when they are selected by gaze. Based on the user's gaze, different features can be activated, so a designer can decide to implement different application reactions depending on whether the user looks at the GazeButton or somewhere else or at another specific area in the application.

Where the user touches Since touch interaction can be used in many different ways and often is the basis for all interaction with tablet computers, where the user touches is another variable in the prototype application that should be considered. Just like with gaze, common touch interaction delivers 2D coordinates but in the case of touch they are always inside the screen and are always obscured by the user's hand. Many functions of the GazeButton are used by touching it and since dwell time and complicated gestures are avoided in the application, all of the new actions involving the gaze button use touch interaction somewhere, so touching is vital.

Where the user looks while touching Considering the two modalities touch and gaze at the same time and keeping in mind the spatial relation to the GazeButton, one gets four variations that can be used for multimodal interaction that involves simultaneous gaze and touch interaction. In most of the interface in the application, when both the user's touch and gaze points are located at the same position, the default pure touch interaction is enabled but when the user touches the GazeButton, the system changes its state depending on where the user looks at while touching the GazeButton. In that case, there are basically two different situations, one being that the user looks at the GazeButton while touching it, in which case a menu can pop up, for instance, the other being that the user looks somewhere other than the GazeButton, in which case a different action can be triggered, depending on whether the user looks at the text area or at the keyboard.

Gestures the user performs In addition to the basic touching and gaze point recognition, gestures can be used to make the GazeButton more expressive. This work's prototype forgoes complicated gaze gestures to keep it simple as they are very unnatural and confusing in comparison to touch gestures that use manual input which the body is used to in terms of controlled movements. The eyes, however, not having evolved into a control organ [46], usually are used only to look at things we are interested in. The used touch gestures on the GazeButton are simple movements like dragging, tapping and holding, of which tapping usually triggers the default action, that is selecting what you are looking at, while holding or double tapping (tapping two times with short delay while keeping the gaze) can be used to select areas the user is looking at. Finally, dragging gestures in basic directions that are started on the GazeButton are used for secondary actions such as mode switching. Using dragging gestures for primary actions could make the interaction annoying and slow as they need more time and effort than tapping, for example.

Areas the user looks at Being the two main features for interaction in the text editing prototype, the combination of where the user touches and where they look provides much functionality but considering only where the user looks consciously, isolated from touch input, leads to another perspective which can be used advantageously and thus is worth thinking about. For instance, the prototype can subtly highlight the key that the user is looking at, whenever the user looks at the keyboard, to give feedback telling the user the computed gaze position and that their gaze is recognized, before the user triggers any action. The gazing area of the user in the application is divided into three main parts that are illustrated in figure 3.1: keyboard, text area and GazeButton. In fact, the system, internally, works with bigger areas than the visible ones to avoid unnecessary errors, for example, when the user's gaze is recognised outside the screen because of limited eye tracker accuracy or precision, and to make it extremely easy to select relatively large objects at screen borders by giving them a big selection area that spreads beyond the screen.

The four interaction modalities are illustrated in figure 1.1. For clarity, this figure represents the GazeButton separated from the target UI instead of integrated into it like in the application. It shows simple combinations of interaction techniques the user can use, depending on the user's aim. One can look at the GazeButton and touch elsewhere or touch the GazeButton and look elsewhere using the same places in the UI but with different interaction methods and triggering different actions. Instead of having two separate parts, UI and GazeButton, in the text editing application, GazeButton and UI are joined seamlessly and the complete operational area for gaze and touch interaction is divided into the three mentioned areas on a higher level.

3.3 Input Interpretation

The input events in the system are received by the input devices' sensors. Of most importance are the touch events and the gaze points, both of them delivered as two-dimensional coordinates. Gaze and touch events differ as the gaze is almost always present without additional info while the user uses the application but touch events often are non-existent when the user does not touch the screen and if they are they correspond to different touch actions so while the gaze input is just a continous stream of gaze points over time, the touch input stream consists of touch events that not only contain where they occured, but also whether the user started to touch the screen, is holding their finger on the screen or released their finger. Furthermore, all of these touch states can correspond to one or more fingers at the same time, even though this multi touch interaction is not used by the prototype text editing application of this thesis, whose input interpretation is described here.

By reason of the limited precision of the eye tracker that makes the received gaze movement quite shaky even if the user keeps looking at the same position, the received gaze points are treated specially as well. To reduce this shakyness, the program always saves the four most recent gaze points by adding every newly received gaze point to a fixed size array [1], replacing the oldest gaze point in the array with it. Then it computes the average x and y value of this four gaze points to build the gaze point that is saved for further calculations and treated as actual gaze input in the program. This intermediate step smoothes the gaze movement in the system but the higher the number of successive gaze points in the array that is used to compute the average, the slower the system's reaction to changes in the user's actual gaze, so there is always a compromise between smoothness and responsiveness. The author finds using four gaze points to be practical, resulting in a compromise that still improves the interaction over just using the most recent gaze point.

---

[1] actually two separate arrays of same length for x and y values

11

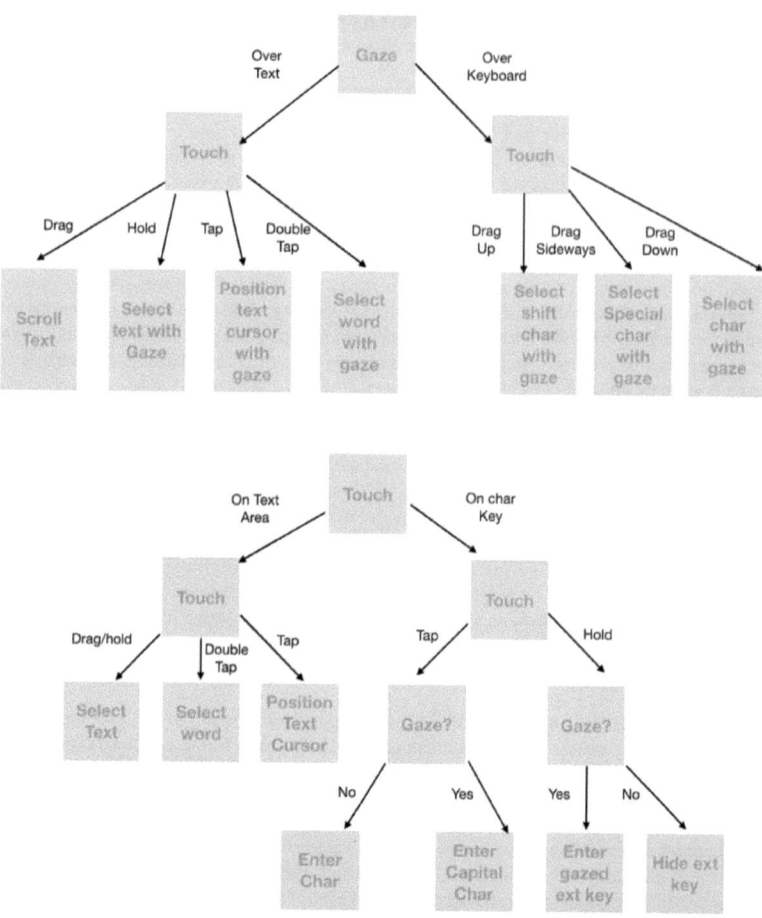

Figure 3.2: Input state models showing considered user interactions of the prototype application and the resulting actions.

Figure 3.2 shows two input state models that depict different user inputs and how they lead to differenct actions after the system's interpretation of them. For all interactions that require timed coordination, a threshold time of 400 ms is used. The author found this amount of time to be very comfortable and it can be changed fast and easily. The selection of characterless keys is omitted in the models as including it would make the model less clear and the reader is informed that it is possible to select characterless keys in the same way as when selecting keys that are mapped to characters. Furthermore, the user always acts according to what they are looking at, whether the system considers gaze data in the user's current interaction or not, so a model from the user's perspective would look different.

The upper input state model corresponds to the top right interaction in figure 1.1. In this model, the current gaze is always considerd in the moment the first touch occurs and the 'Touch' in this model always means a touch on the GazeButton. While the model starts with 'Gaze', to the software, the meaningful interaction always starts with touch as for this model, leaving the user the freedom to watch wherever they like in the UI without changing the application state.

In the left branch of the upper model the user looks somewhere in the text area while touching the GazeButton, for example at a word they like to remove. If the user then quickly releases the finger from the GazeButton without touching it again within 400 ms, a 'Tap' is recognised and the software places the cursor at the position between two characters in the text area that is nearest to the user's gaze point. However, if the user touches the GazeButton and releases their finger twice within 400 ms, a 'Double Tap' is recognised, resulting in selecting the whole word the user is looking at for further manipulation. Moreover, if the user touches and holds the touch on the GazeButton while looking at the text area, they can either scroll the text by moving the finger on the screen considerably or they can keep their finger on its position on the GazeButton and move their gaze direction to freely select a portion of the text in the text area. In this gaze selection mode, the start of the selected text is the position between two characters in the text area that has been nearest to the user's gaze point on the screen when they started touching the GazeButton and the end of the selected text is determined in the same way but when the user releases their finger from the GazeButton. Then, all text between the start and end point of the gaze selection is selected. The explicit start end end of the selection by touch is used to avoid dwell time or complicated eye gestures.

In the right branch of the upper model, every interaction is started by the user by looking at the keyboard while touching the GazeButton. In this case, the touch on the GazeButton has to be held in order to trigger an action. It would be possible to add another function here by just holding the touch position and using gaze but the prototype only uses drag gestures for starting an action at this point to avoid unwanted actions. When the user then drags the finger farther than a specified threshold distance, the main drag direction is computed, whereby only basic x and y coordinate distances are used to determine this direction, resulting in the four possible main directions top, bottom, left and right, where 'left and right', that could be used for different actions, are simply considered the same direction in the system, called 'sideways' in the model, so three different actions can be performed depending on the main drag direction that corresponds to a specific selection mode:

Shift character selection mode   When the user's drag is mostly towards the top of the screen, the system switches to this mode, changing all of the displayed characters on the on-screen keyboard to their corresponding shift characters.

Special character selection mode   Has the user's drag been mainly to the left or mainly to the right, the displayed keyboard changes temporarily into another keyboard that only shows special characters such as '*' or '@'.

Normal character selection mode   If the user's drag has been mostly to the bottom of the screen, the displayed characters on the keyboard do not change.

After the user dragged further than the threshold distance, the software switches to one of the three eye selection modes. Once having entered one of this modes, every key the user's gaze is recognised on is highlighted strongly and its corresponding character (if any) is entered at the current cursor position in the text area if the user releases their finger from the GazeButton. Independent from which gaze selection mode the user is in, they always can select one of the visible characters/keys on the keyboard, that always include characterless keys like backspace. After one key is selected, the system returns to its initial state, being ready for the next action, so to eye type more than one character, the user has to enter an eye selection mode multiple times.

The lower input state model starts with 'Touch', meaning that the gaze direction does not matter in the beginning of the corresponding interaction. Similar to the upper input state model, in this model, the interaction begins with a touch on either the text area or the keyboard, where on the keyboard always a character key is touched.

When the user touches the text area, gaze is not considered until they remove their finger from the screen, leading to pure touch text interaction corresponding to the left branch of the lower model. The user then can either release the finger without dragging it on the screen to position the text cursor or they can hold and drag their finger to select text between the point where the touch began and the point where it is released. Additionally, if the user touched a word and released the finger without dragging, they can, related to the word selection in the upper input state model, perform a 'Double Tap' by touching the same word again within 400 ms to not only position the cursor, which always happens after the first tap, but also select the word at cursor position.

In the corresponding interaction to the right branch of the lower model, the user touches on a character key on the on-screen keyboard and then holds their finger on the screen for 400 ms or releases their finger before. Now, in the next level of the model, in the left branch, the system tests whether the user is looking at the GazeButton but in the right branch it tests whether the user looks near an extension key that appeared after holding the touch. If the user releases their finger in a timely manner (before 400 ms or an other determined threshold time is over) a 'Tap' is recognised by the software and, depending on whether the user looked at the GazeButton or somewhere else while releasing the finger, a capital character or a standard character corresponding to the touched key is entered at cursor position in the text area. For better understanding: If the user looks at the GazeButton at this moment, all the characters on the keys are, visually and internally in the system, changed into their corresponding shift characters, so looking at the GazeButton is like pressing and holding shift on a physical keyboard and this 'gaze shift' can be used while typing conventionally through touch. Touch typing with pure gaze shift corresponds to the interaction in the bottom left of figure 1.1.

If the user touches a character key and holds the touch for at least 400 ms, 'extension keys' appear. Those are temporally displayed keys, other than that, similar to the standard keys, that contain a special character each that is related to the touched key they belong to. They are arranged like a radial menu around the touched key, enabling the user to select them easily by gaze. While still holding the finger on the touched standard key, the user can either look near an extension key and release their finger to enter the special character corresponding to the extension key at cursor position in the text area, or they can look away from the extension keys while releasing their finger, in which case nothing is entered and the system returns to its initial state. An example of the mentioned extension keys in the text editing application can be seen in figure 3.3.

The described and implemented novel interaction possibilities are easy to use and understand and require only minimal movement, using gaze and one extra button, the GazeButton. Theoretically, one could use the prototype to write, delete and edit text by just moving the eyes and one finger but it was built to contribute to improving conventional typing on tablet PCs instead of replacing it.

A finished version of the gaze enhanced text editing application would probably not need all functions that are implemented in the prototype. The goal here is much more the demonstration of all the functions in a single program, than completeness, although it is good to know that all of the interaction techniques can be used in the same software without interfering with each other.

3.4 Complementary interaction modalities

This section describes interaction modalities of the text editing prototype software, ordered by desired outcome, pointing out implemented alternatives that can be combined to achieve this outcome.

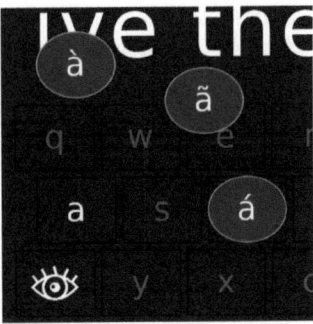

Figure 3.3: The standard key 'a' and its corresponding extension keys after touching and holding 'a' for 400 ms. When the extension keys appear, all other keys are darkened to make it easier for the user to concentrate on the extension keys when selecting one of them through gaze.

3.4.1 Typing

Typing with the protoype can be done with pure touch typing on the soft keyboard that is displayed on the screen, pure gaze based typing with touch for mode switching and confirmation and with any combination of both. In addition, if a physical keyboard is connected to the tablet, this can be used for input as well, although this has not been described earlier in this thesis as the focus lies on handheld devices, in particular tablets, and most tablet PCs are not used with a physical keyboard that would make them less portable, even though it is usually possible to connect one via Bluetooth or an USB On-The-Go cable. All together, there are three ways of typing in the text editing application:

1) Typing with a physical keyboard   While typing with a physical keyboard is usually the fastest typing method with good haptic feedback, in the field of mobile devices it is often not practical. The reason why this option is still mentioned in this thesis and implemented in the application is that sometimes a physical keyboard is nevertheless used with handheld devices and there is no reason not to adapt the application to those situations if this adaption is done in a way that does not interfere with the main usage, which is the case, and if even then functions of the prototype application might be beneficial. For example, one might like to gaze select extension keys that can not be typed on a standard physical keyboard, combining eye typing with classic typing. As the main intention of the prototype is to show possibilities, it is legitimate to consider the possibilty that only one function of it is used as a daily help. For example, the user could type with an external keyboard if they are temporarily at a place where it can be used comfortably and use the gaze function only for text selection using the control key on the keyboard instead of the on-screen gaze button for very fast word selection.

2) Touch typing on the screen   Touch typing, meaning to use ones fingers to tap at letters on an on-screen keyboard which results in entering them, has become the dominant typing and general interaction method on mobile devices like tablet PCs and smartphones, in most cases using projected capacitive touch technology enabling practically unlimited multi-touch [1].

This typing method can theoretically be very fast but suffers from low ergonomics and a feedback that leaves much to be desired. Feedback during touch typing on a flat screen is often limited to the displayed entered letters in the text area, especially on most tablets, on which this thesis focusses, that do not offer the option to vibrate for haptic feedback when entering a letter like many smartphones do. It is often impossible to see a letter on the screen while typing it, because the finger obscures it, which is no problem on a physical keyboard where you can feel the keys before typing them but on a touch screen this haptic feedback while touching a key without pressing it is missing making it hard to know which key one is on as there are no physical boundaries between keys. Moreover, typing on the screen in most cases requires the user to hold one or both of their arms relatively high which can result in high physical effort, in particular when holding the tablet at the same time.

Despite all those problems, touch typing has its raison d'être for needing only software and a touch screen that is provided anyway, keeping mobile devices very portable, so it is included in the prototype and works in the usual way.

3) Eye Typing   Eye typing in the prototype application differs from standalone eye typing solutions that have already been discussed in this thesis as it is meant to be solely an extension of conventional typing, analogous to the GazeButton concept being an extension to existing UIs and interactions. In the application, whenever they like the user can enter any character by eye typing using relaxed finger gestures on one of the GazeButtons as explained earlier in this thesis. While limiting typing to this technique is probably too cumbersome, it might be convenient for small text corrections, for instance, in combination with gaze text selection to remove a word[2] without having to move a whole arm.

As, among others, the last example showed, the real benefit of the application lies in combining the new functions with old ones.

3.4.2 Text Selection

Text selection, together with typing, completes the basic functions of a text editor since backspace can be entered just as any other key and thus, in this thesis, removing text counts as typing. Similar to typing, text selection in the prototype text editor can be fulfilled conventionally with the keyboard or the touchscreen alone or by using gaze based interaction. Because scrolling is needed to select a currently invisible part of a large body of text it will also be discussed here. There are several ways of selecting text in the application:

Keyboard.   When the user selects text with the physical keyboard they would probably be relatively slow compared to the other methods. That is why this selection method could greatly benefit from combining it with gaze selection. Nevertheless, one benefit would be that with normal keyboard selection that is implemented in the prototype using shift and the arrow keys, the user can select single characters extremely reliably which is not possible with fingers on the screen or the eyes in the way those methods normally are implemented and also in the way they are implemented in the text editing application of this thesis. To select text with a physical keyboard in the application, the user can move the text cursor with the arrow keys and select areas by holding shift, moving the arrow keys and releasing shift.

Touch Screen.   When the user selects text with a finger on the screen it might feel rather natural because the user gets visual feedback at the location they touch. The bodily problems, though, are about the same as with touch typing, maybe even graver because the text area is located at the upper part of the screen and holding the arm higher is more strenuous. In most touch screen text editors the text selection starts by selecting the whole word the user touched long enough (dwell time based) and showing two anchors, one at the beginning of the selected text and one at the end. Then those anchors can be moved separately to select a coherent part of the text. However, the

---

[2]backspace can be selected with a normal eye typing gesture, just like the character keys

prototype application uses a different technique for selecting text areas with touch without dwell time where the user just has to touch and hold at the beginning of the selection, drag the finger to the end of the selection and release the finger. Usually, the dwell time for text selection is needed in pure touch screen interaction on mobile devices to still be able to scroll the text comfortably by touching it anywhere and because a scroll bar would be too small for reliable touch selection or would take much room on the screen. In the prototype application, firstly, scrolling is done by a gesture on the GazeButton so dwell time is not needed and secondly, the text is made bigger for gaze selection which results in a very precise touch selection in relation to the font size where corrections of the selection are not needed most of the time. Cursor positioning as well as word selection is still possible by single or double tapping.

Eyes.   When the user selects text with the eyes they can be relatively fast when compared to the other methods, without obscuring any of the text and with minimal physical effort. Text selection and cursor positioning in the application can be done with the eyes and the gaze button just like with the finger on the screen by holding, tapping or double tapping on the gaze button and moving ones gaze over the text area. The only possible disadvantage of this type of text selection is the limited precision of the eye tracker. However, the text can be made bigger which has been done in the prototype or if a physical keyboard is used one could implement the option to adjust the final gaze selection with the keyboard combining the high speed of the eyes for big area selection with the complete precision of the keyboard for fine tuning.

Selecting with a mouse, which also is possible on most handheld devices is not discussed here because it is even less common with handheld mobile devices than using an external keyboard.

3.5   Implementation

The hardware platform the prototype is implemented on is a Surface Pro 3 tablet running 64-bit Windows 10 Pro with an Intel Core i5-4300U CPU at a ground frequenzy of 1,9 GHz and 4 GB of RAM. For eye tracking a Tobii 4C eye tracker with 90 Hz and embedded processing to reduce CPU load [32] is placed at the bottom center of the tablet's screen in widescreen orientation using the self-adhesive magnetic plate that comes with it. This is the placement the eye tracker has been designed for.

On the software side, Java with Processing and the eclipse IDE are used because it is more powerful and seems more convenient to the author than the Processing IDE. The on-screen keyboard had to be implemented anew to be able to add new features to the keys and use them with both touch and gaze but as the new functions should be seen as an extension of existing interaction methods the implemented keyboard layout is almost identical to the standard keyboard on the surface pro tablet in terms of character/key locations, proportions and colors. In the text area, every character is a distinct java object to be able to easily find positions between them and place the cursor there when needed. To achieve that the gaze based interaction in the text area is as precise as possible, a rather big font size of screen height divided by 8 is used. Moreover, in order to make the application work and function independent from the resolution of the used screen, almost all dimensions used in the code are derived from the pixel based screen width and screen height of the device the application is running on.

Figure 3.4: Feedback showing gazed cursor position (top) or gazed key (bottom): subtle grey while looking around (left) and more obvious green during meaningful interaction (right)

3.6   Feedback

When pointing with a mouse cursor or touching on the screen there is always at least the visual feedback in form of the cursor on the screen or a haptic hint when feeling the screen with the finger. When interacting with the eyes, feedback like that is missing and an 'eye cursor' would be annoying because one does not always want to point with the eyes wherefore extra unobtrusive visual feedback is important with gaze based interaction, in particular to users that are not familiar with this kind of interaction and very unsure if the system understands their eye movement correctly. That is why, in the prototype application, there is always visual feedback indicating where the system recognises the user's gaze or rather where an action would take place if the user triggered one with the current gaze, even before the user starts a manipulative action.

There are two types of visual gaze feedback in the application, an unobtrusive subtle one and a very obvious one. Both are illustrated in figure 3.4. When the user only looks anywhere in the application without starting a manipulative action, a subtle grey text cursor or a grey frame around a key indicates which object or position the gaze is recognised on, depending on whether the user looks at the keyboard or at the text area. This subtle grey feedback is clearly perceivable without disturbing a look around too much when it has no further intention. However, if the user starts an action by, for example, looking at the text area and holding a touch on the GazeButton or looking at the keyboard and performing a drag gesture on the GazeButton, the feedback color changes into a more obvious light green, and in the case of gazed key feedback the whole background color of the key the user is looking at is changed into green instead of only the border color of the key into grey. This feedback design allows conspicuous feedback to be displayed only when needed.

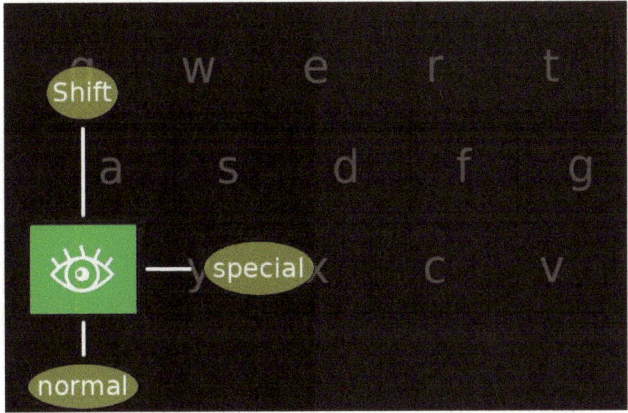

Figure 3.5: After holding the GazeButton long enough, all the other keys are darkened and this visual assistance appears indicating the three possible eye typing modes and the corresponding drag directions to start them.

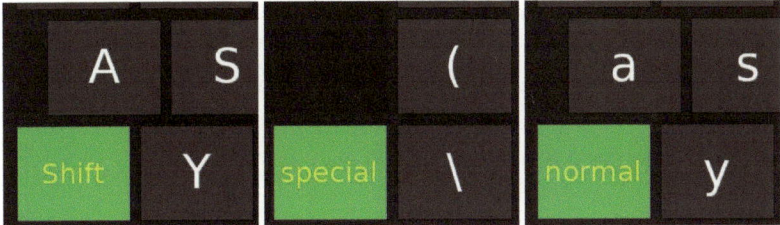

Figure 3.6: If the user entered an eye typing mode by performing a drag gesture on the GazeButton, depending on the mode the user has entered, the GazeButton shows if the user is expected to eye type a shift character (left), a special character (middle) or a standard character (right)

Additionally, as illustrated in figure 3.5, when the user holds a touch on the GazeButton, after 500 ms a visual help is displayed showing the user in which direction they have to drag to start the desired one of the three eye typing modes. The longer 500 ms in contrast to the usual 400 ms in the program are used to reduce the risk of hindering the interaction of users that are familiar with the functions because the displayed help is only useful for inexperienced users and annoying for experienced ones. As illustrated in figure 3.6, after the user entered an eye typing mode by dragging, the visual appearance of the GazeButton changes to indicate which eye typing mode the user is in. As soon as the user leaves the eye typing mode, the GazeButton's appearance returns to default, showing an eye symbol again.

3.7 Interaction Technique Examples

In this section, implemented interaction examples involving gaze interaction are presented along with photographs of the running application with a user.

3.7.1   Touch typing with 'gaze shift'

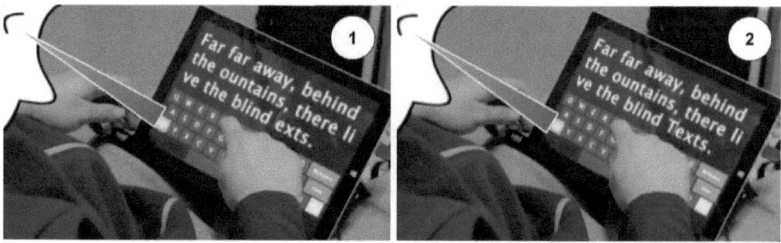

Figure 3.7: The user enters a capital letter by looking at the GazeButton while tapping a letter key on the on-screen keyboard.

In figure 3.7 the user would like to enter a capital 'T' to build the word 'Texts', wherefore they already set the cursor at the right position. Then the user simply looks at the GazeButton which changes all the characters on the on-screen keyboard into their corresponding shift characters (1) and taps at the 'T' while still looking at the GazeButton. The 'T' is entered at cursor position (2) and the user did not have to move their arm more than when entering a lowercase 't'.

3.7.2   Gaze based cursor positioning

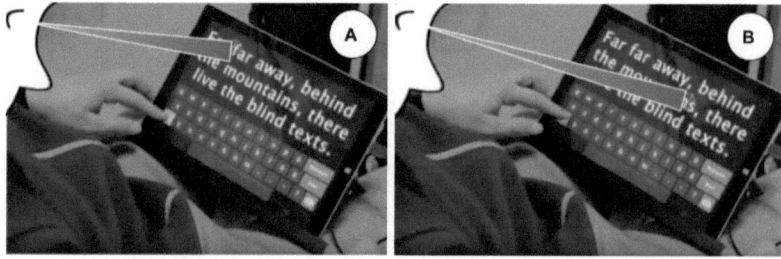

Figure 3.8: By looking at the desired position and tapping the GazeButton, the user places the text cursor.

As illustrated in figure 3.8 the user can set the text cursor with a tap on the GazeButton. In the first example, the user looks between the first space and the 'f' in 'Far far away' and places the cursor there when tapping the GazeButton (A). In the second example, the user acts similarly when placing the cursor between the last 'n' and the 's' of the word 'mountains' (B).

3.7.3   Gaze based word selection

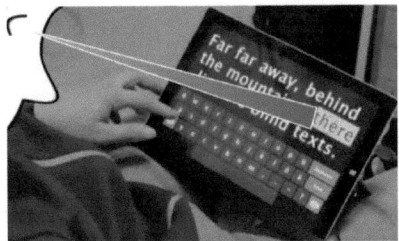

Figure 3.9: The user selects the word at gaze position with a double tap on the GazeButton.

Selecting a word gaze based is similar to gaze based cursor positioning. The user looks anywhere in the word 'there' while tapping two times on the GazeButton within 400 ms, performing a double tap. This is illustrated in figure 3.9.

3.7.4   Free text area selection with gaze

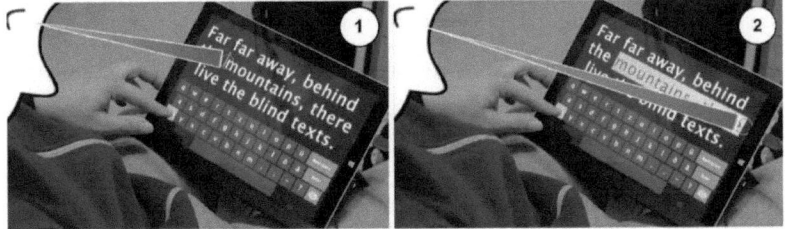

Figure 3.10: The user selects a text area freely with the eyes while holding the GazeButton.

In figure 3.10 the user selects the text fragment 'mountains, there'. First, the user looks at the beginning of the word 'mountains' while touching the GazeButton to place the cursor there and start a gaze based free text area selection (1). Then they keep holding the GazeButton while moving their gaze to the end of the word 'there' to select the targeted text area (2) and release the touch to finish the selection.

3.7.5 Eye typing a special character

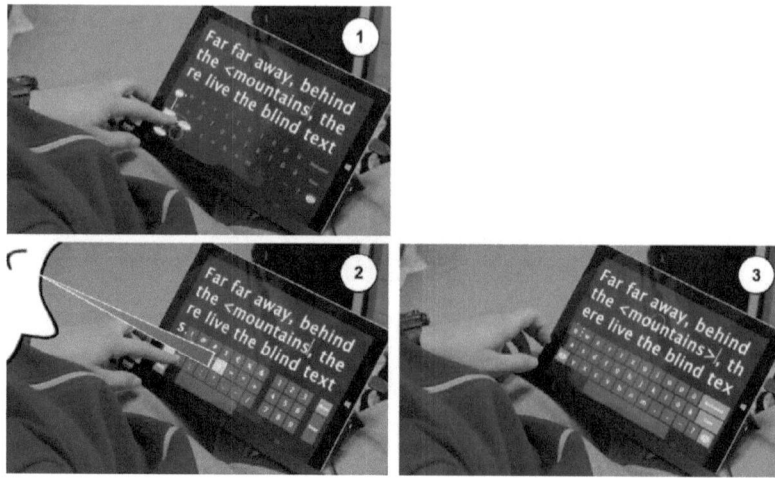

Figure 3.11: The user enters an angle bracket with eye typing.

In figure 3.11 the user would like to enclose the word 'mountains' in angle brackets for what the user already has entered the left angle bracket and set the text cursor to the desired position for entering the right bracket. Now the user touches the GazeButton and holds it for 500 ms until the assistance of figure 3.5 appears (1). The holding is optional and the user could start a drag gesture immediately without waiting until the assistance appears. Then the user drags sideways without releasing the touch to enter the special character eye typing mode resulting in a keyboard switch to the special character keyboard (2). To finish their task the user looks at the key with the right angle bracket (2) and releases the touch while doing so to enter the bracket. After releasing the touch the keyboard returns to its default and the gazed character (the right angle bracket) is entered (3).

3.7.6 Selecting extension keys with gaze

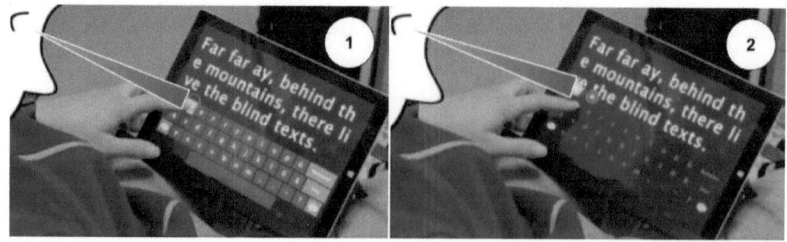

Figure 3.12: The user selects an extension key of the 'w' key with gaze.

In figure 3.12 the user at first holds the 'w' key and also looks at it although the gaze is not considered in the system at this point (1). After 400 ms of holding the key, its corresponding two extension keys appear of which the user selects the left one by looking at it and releasing the touch (2). Because the 'w' only has two extension keys they appear above it on the screen at the same height. If a key has more than two extension keys, like the 'a' key in figure 3.3 they are arranged circularly similar to a radial menu but at positions where no obscuring hand is expected to enable the user to select them fast and easily with gaze.

4   User Study: Word Selection

To compare novel gaze based interaction with its conventional touch only counterpart a user study has been conducted and is described in this section.

4.1   Study Design

In order to test whether the GazeButton can achieve the goal of improving text interaction, it was decided to limit the study to one of the new interaction techniques in order to make the study easier to carry out for both the participants and the researcher. The chosen technique to be compared with its classic touch only alternative is the gaze based free text area selection (shown in figure 3.10) as the author found this technique to be the most promising.

The author attended many meetings at the university to plan the study and find out which technique to use as a classic alternative for comparison with the gaze based text selection and how to implement the software for the study. As a result both the gaze and the touch selection used for the study have been changed from character based to word based since it is much more common to select whole words than parts of them and the touch selection on android devices, for example, is usually word based as well so the gaze based one should be, too, for a fair comparison.

Figure 4.1: The beginning of a touch text selection with anchors in the user study software after the user touched a word (in this example the word 'of') for 400 ms.

Furthermore, the touch selection in the study is different from the one implemented in the prototype application, not only because it is word based. It also uses dwell time and anchors in order to simulate the standard text selection on handheld mobile devices so to select text with touch only interaction in the software for the study, the user touches the text for 400 ms, then two anchors appear as shown in figure 4.1 at the touched word which is also selected and the user touches and moves those anchors by dragging to change the selected text area.

The gaze based text selection in the user study software is the same as in the prototype application with the only change being that it is word based instead of character based so the words at the start and the end of the gaze selection path are always selected completely.

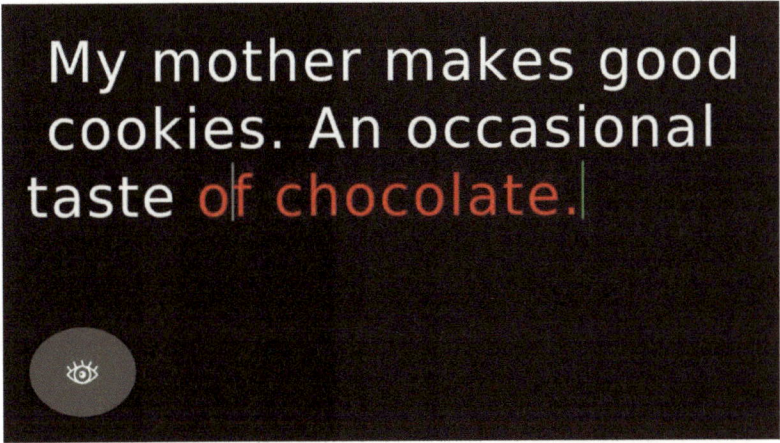

Figure 4.2: The reduced user interface at the beginning of a selection task with 'big text' as used in the gaze selection tasks of the study. In the touch selection tasks there is no text cursor or GazeButton.

In every repetition of the study the participant selects a coherent area of the displayed text that is selected randomly but always begins at the start and ends at the end of a word to fit the word based selection techniques. The text that should be selected is marked by red font color. When the user has selected the marked text correctly the next repetition starts automatically. To investigate the influence of font size on the two selection tasks, that are either the gaze based one or touch only, two font sizes are used, one being the one of the prototype application that is called 'big text' the other being half of this font size, called 'small text'. With the variable of font size there are four conditions for the selection tasks in the user study:

1. Gaze with big text

2. Touch with big text

3. Gaze with small text

4. Touch with small text

For each of these conditions, the participant at first does 5 repetitions/text selections, as described above, without data logging to get accustomed to the task and then does 50 more repetitions while data is logged to get accurate results. The condition order a participant gets is counter balanced where every next participant gets the next condition order of the following two-dimensional array: { 1, 3, 2, 4 }, { 3, 1, 4, 2 }, { 2, 4, 3, 1 }, { 4, 2, 1, 3 }, { 2, 4, 1, 3 }, { 4, 2, 3, 1 }, { 3, 1, 2, 4 }, { 1, 3, 4, 2 }

Both gaze tasks and both touch tasks are always directly consecutive inside a sequence. Other than that, the order is randomized which resulted in eight distinct sequences.

To get generalizable results the selection paragraphs for each repetition are built using the 500 phrases from MacKenzie and Soukoreff [18] with least possible redundancy. To have approximately the same visual amount of text in all four conditions, two of those phrases are combined for the conditions with big text and eight for those with small text. Furthermore, for a more realistic look, all phrases are manipulated so that they start with a capital letter and end with a period.

The hardware used in the study is exactly the same as the one for the text editing prototype application and the user study software has been developed on basis of the prototype software after removing the keyboard and most of the functionality since in the user study, the GazeButton is the only needed key of the original application's keyboard. The interface is illustrated in figure 4.2 and is nearly the same in all conditions of the study.

The following data is logged by the user study software for every repetition:

- condition number (1-4)

- repetition number (1-50; reset for every condition)

- number of finished wrong selections made by the user in the repetition

- time the user needed to select the target text in milliseconds

- displayed text of the repetition

- target text of the repetition (the red text that has to be selected)

- index of the first and the last character of the target text in the String of the displayed text

- pixel coordinates of the center of the first and the last character of the target text

The following data is logged for every frame (about 1/30 of a second) of each repetition:

- elapsed time in milliseconds since the start of the study software

- current touch event, if any, consisting of pixel coordinates and action (touch, hold or release) of the touch

- pixel coordinates of the current gaze point (can be outside the screen)

With the logged data, the participants' perfomance can be evaluated and reconstructed.

4.2   Participants

For counter balancing the study has been conducted with 16 participants which is a multiple of the number of possible condition orders. Exactly half of the participants are female, the other half male. Their age ranged from 17 to 52 years, of which 13 were 26 years old or younger with the majority of 11 participants being between 21 and 26 years old. Most participants used neither glasses nor contact lenses while 3 participants used glasses, 2 used contact lenses and one used one contact lens. Fourteen participants were right-handed, the others left-handed. Thirteen participants stated to have much experience with touch interaction (at least 4 on a scale of 1 through 5) and also thirteen stated to have no or very little experience with eye gaze interaction (2 or less on a scale of 1 through 5).

4.3   Study Procedure

For each participant, after they was explained the purpose of the study and they completed a questionnaire about demographics, they sat at a table in front of the tablet in a relaxed position and the eye tracker has been calibrated to their eyes. Then they went through the following procedure for each of the four conditions:

1. 5 text selections with instructions to learn the task

2. 50 text selections with voluntary breaks after every 10 repetitions, in which data logging is paused and the program informs the participant about their progress

3. filling out a questionnaire to evaluate the task

An example picture for each task is shown in figure 4.3. After the participant finished all four tasks they filled out one last questionnaire in which they ordered the four tasks by preference and gave reasons for their decision.

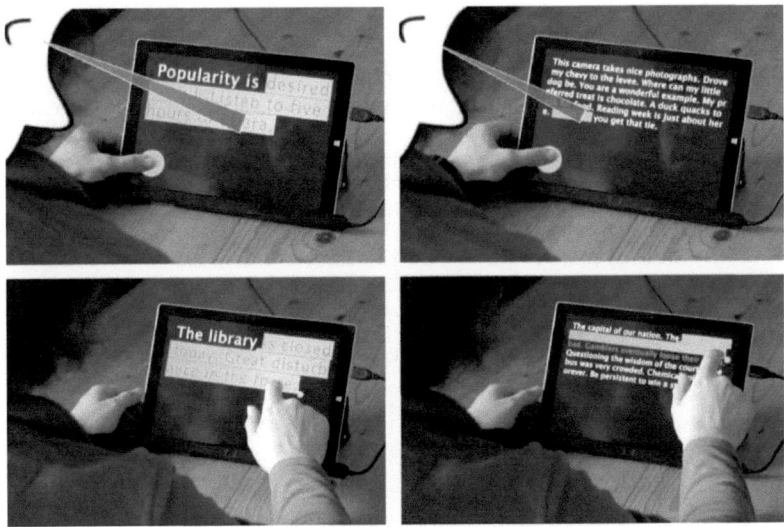

Figure 4.3: A user performing a selection in all four tasks of the study. Gaze tasks at the top, touch tasks at the bottom, tasks with big font size on the left, tasks with small font size on the right.

5 Results

In this section the results of the user study are presented, including the participants' qualitative feedback.

5.1 Performance

A repeated measures ANOVA was conducted to examine the effect of font size and interaction technique (gaze or touch) on average time needed per repetition/text selection in the user study. Because of significance in Mauchly's sphericity test the results were corrected after Greenhouse-Geisser. For the time needed per text selection the following results have been found:

For the main effect interaction technique there were no statistically significant differences at $F(1,13) = .645$ and $p = 0.436$ but for the main effect font size significant differences have been found at $F(1,13) = 24.520$ and $p < .001$. With the bigger font size the users were significantly faster, which is an expected result.

Between the effects of interaction technique and font size there was a statistically significant interaction at $F(1,13) = 10.068$ and $p = .007$. Because of this significant interaction pairwise post hoc comparisons with Bonferroni corrections have been conducted and lead to the following results:

1. In the selection tasks with small font size, the participants were significantly faster with touch selection than with gaze selection ($p = .045$).

2. In the selection tasks with big font size, there was no significant difference between the interaction techniques ($p = .087$).

3. In the gaze selection tasks, the participants were significantly faster with the big text font ($p = .001$).

4. In the touch selection tasks, the participants were significantly faster with the small text font ($p = .038$), whereby this effect was less pronounced than the one in the gaze selection tasks.

5.2 Questionnaires and Feedback

In addition to the demographics questionnaire whose results have been presented in section 4.2 the users filled out a performance questionnaire for every of the four tasks in which they rated the learnability, ease, physical effort, eye tiredness, precision and speed they felt on a scale of 1 to 5, and a ranking questionnaire in which the participants ordered the four selection tasks by their preference, where the favourite task is placed at rank 1 and the least favourite at rank 4.

Figure 5.1 shows the number of times every task has been placed on rank 1 by the participants. While the gaze selection task with big text is favoured over all the other tasks by 10 out of 16 participants, the gaze selection task with small text has been placed on every of the four ranks exactly the same amount of times. Furthermore, the gaze selection task with big text is the only one that has never been placed on rank 4 and the touch selection task with small text is the only one that has never been placed on rank 1. Overall, the ranking shows that participants prefer gaze selection when the font size is big.

In the performance questionnaire the participants rated six aspects for each selection task:

Learnability All participants except two found all four tasks easy to learn, rating the learnabilty of them at least 4 out of 5. The four times the learnability of a task has been rated lower than 4 out of 5 include two times the touch task with small text (rated 3) and both of the gaze tasks (rated 3 for big and 2 for small text).

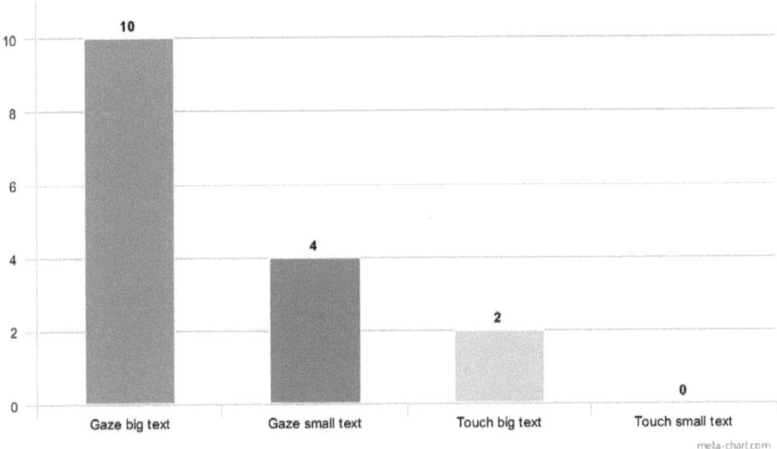

Figure 5.1: The four conditions of the study and the number of times they have been placed on rank 1 by the participants in the user study.

Ease   Like the learnability, the felt ease to perform the tasks has been rated high throughout all four tasks, namely at least 4 out of 5 in 54 of the 64 ratings. The 10 lower ratings contain one time 2 out of 5 for the touch task with small text and 10 times 3 out of 5, of which three are for the touch tasks, six are for the gaze task with small text and one is for the gaze task with big text so there might be a tendency to find the gaze task with small text harder than the other tasks.

Physical Effort   During the study most participants pointed out that the touch selection is much more physically demanding than the gaze selection, with the small text gaze selection still being more physically demanding than the one with big text. This also reflected in the performance questionnaires where, in the gaze tasks, 14 out of the 16 participants rated the aspect 'No Physical Effort' in the task with big text at least 4 out of 5 while in the task with small text 12 participants rated the same aspect at least 4 out of 5. In the touch tasks, however, with big text, only 6 participants rated the physical ease at least 4 out of 5 and with small text only 5 gave this rating.

Eye Tiredness   As for eye tiredness, the participants tended to find the gaze tasks more tiring for their eyes than the touch tasks. Out of the 64 ratings concerning the aspect 'No Eye Tiredness' that the 16 participants gave for the four tasks, 46 were at least 4 out of 5, of which only 18 were for a gaze task and the rest for a touch task. Out of the 18 lower ratings for this aspect, 11 were 3 out of 5, of which two were for both touch tasks and the rest distributed evenly among both gaze tasks, and 7 were 2 out of 5, of which four were for the gaze task with small text, one for the gaze task with big text and two for both touch tasks.

Precision   The participants tended to feel the gaze selection to be less precise than the touch selection. While the 32 touch task ratings for precision were all but four at least 4 out of 5, the 32 gaze task ratings contain 15 ratings that are lower, of which two are 2 out of 5 for both gaze tasks and 13 are 3 out of 5, namely nine for the gaze task with small text and four for the gaze task with big text.

Speed   Both the gaze and the touch tasks felt fast to perform to the participants. Out of the 64 speed ratings, 50 were 4 or 5 out of 5, of which the 33 4 out of 5 ratings were distributed relatively evenly among all four tasks with a higher proportion of touch task ratings, while the 17 5 out of 5 ratings were only two times for the gaze task with small text, eight times for the gaze task with big text and about the same amount of times for both touch tasks. The 14 lower than 4 ratings were distributed about evenly among the four tasks, with the only two ratings that were as low as 2 out of 5 being for the gaze and touch tasks with small text.

In the following are some statements participants made in the ranking questionnaire:

- *Eye tracking was way faster and felt smoother, especially with big text - touch selection sometimes was slightly more precise but definitely more stressful / strainful.*

- *Favourite (Gaze big text): Speed, no physical effort, but easier than with small text; touch is a bit tiring and feels slower, gaze is easy but not that precise*

- *bigger* (text) *is easier and faster, gaze is a bit less precise*

- *Mir gefällt die Blickauswahl besser, weil es etwas besonderes ist und es angenehmer für den Arm ist. Ich finde die kleinen Texte besser, weil man da mehr auf einmal sieht.*

- *Mit den Augen ungewohnt aber angenehmer, weil man nicht mit dem Finger rummachen muss. Man muss dafür mehr üben als für touch. Mit großem Text ist es nicht so anstrengend.*

- *Auswahl der Augen generell bevorzugt, weil keine physische Anstrengung, small text auf Ranking 1, weil dies die lustigere Herausforderung war*

- *selecting the big text by looking at it is much easier because i did not have to think so much where i was looking, but rather just look at the start and end word and the sentence was selected. With the small text, I had to focus more specifically at the begging of the word i want to start selecting from. However I believe that with more practice this will not be a problem, since i have been using touch selection for much longer time.*

- *kleiner Text schlechter weil schwieriger auszuwählen; gaze auf 1 weil dabei im Gegensatz zu touch der Arm nicht weh tut*

6 Discussion

In the user Study, participants have not been significantly faster with gaze based selection than with touch only selection but still it is very obvious that they prefer gaze selection over touch selection when the text is big enough and also are not slower with gaze than with touch when this is the case. One reason for that clear preference is most likely that they felt much more comfortable with the gaze selection in terms of physical ease. However, with the small font size, the participants were significantly slower with gaze, compared to touch, which indicates that the precision of the eye selection is not yet optimal for small objects.

Because of the new gaze selection's superiority over touch selection in terms of physical comfort and screen visibility and its only disadvantage being the precision of the eye tracking, the author thinks that, provided that the precision and availability of eye tracking will increase, there is great potential in improving interaction by using gaze based techniques. Considering that even beginners are not slower with gaze selection than with touch only selection, with more training of the user, gaze selection might even outperform touch selection in terms of speed. Even though some participants clearly found the gaze selection to be less precise than the touch selection and there is a need to improve gaze estimation precision, the user acceptance seems already to be there, especially concerning gaze interaction with large objects. Only the availability of both gaze based interaction and its corresponding hardware is still relatively low but will probably keep rising as it has in the past.

Furthermore, the GazeButton has only been used in a text editing application although its aim can be seen more generally. It can be used in many different fields as a basis for enhancing or experimenting with interaction that exploits evolving eye tracking technology in a straightforward way. Integrated into an UI it is an area with high functionality density that can be used anytime to shortcut many interactions.

For example, in a web browser, the GazeButton might be used to zoom with a one finger gesture on it where the zoom is carried out at gaze location or to set the focus to a text field in a form by a simple tap while looking at the text field. On mobile devices the GazeButton could be used independently from other apps throughout the system to simply enable one-handed interaction with full screen reachability by linking every touch on it to the gaze position. In desktop environments various mouse gestures can be performed on it instead of touch gestures or there could even be some dedicated hardware for the GazeButton like a touchpad on the keyboard.

Only a small part of the GazeButton's potential has been put into practice and even so, it already proved to be beneficial in some situations. The author believes that much more that is yet to be investigated can be achieved with this powerful interaction hub.

7 Conclusion

The GazeButton extends the conventional button concept with progressive gaze based interactions. Its concept and corresponding possible usage for gaze based interaction with touch has been presented and reflected on in this thesis. Additionally, a text editing application has been developed to demonstrate the new interaction techniques with working examples on a tablet computer, proving that they are feasible, and a second application based on the first one has been developed and collected valuable information in a user study where it has been used to test the performance and feeling of the new gaze based text selection and compare it with conventional touch text selection. The user study signified that eye tracking technology is already sophisticated enough to be used to improve conventional touch interaction at least in terms of comfort and that user acceptance is already there.

In future work, one might try to improve the new interaction techniques, take them as inspiration and compare more of them with the older alternatives through user studies as the presented study only covered a small part of the GazeButton's possibilities. Moreover, the new techniques might be adapted to smartphones where the screen is very small and text interaction is especially cumbersome, or they might be used on a desktop PC, adapted to keyboard usage, just to have fast and pleasant interaction alternatives. There is much material for further research.

Contents of the enclosed CD

- Electronic version of the thesis in the original format (LaTex) and in PDF format

- The prototype application with source code

- The user study software, that is based on the prototype, with source code

- Logged data of the user study software

- Results of the user study questionnaires in CSV format

- Videos showing a user while using one of the applications

- Sources cited in the paper that are available in electronic form

Origin of illustrations

All figures with the exception of figure 5.1, which was produced by meta-chart.com, were created by myself.

References

[1] Gary Barrett and Ryomei Omote. Projected-capacitive touch technology. *Information Display*, 26(3):16–21, 2010.

[2] Joanna Bergstrom-Lehtovirta and Antti Oulasvirta. Modeling the functional area of the thumb on mobile touchscreen surfaces. In *Proceedings of the SIGCHI Conference on Human Factors in Computing Systems*, pages 1991–2000. ACM, 2014.

[3] Richard A Bolt. Gaze-orchestrated dynamic windows. In *ACM SIGGRAPH Computer Graphics*, volume 15, pages 109–119. ACM, 1981.

[4] Andreas Bulling and Hans Gellersen. Toward mobile eye-based human-computer interaction. *IEEE Pervasive Computing*, 9(4):8–12, 2010.

[5] Lung-Pan Cheng, Hsiang-Sheng Liang, Che-Yang Wu, and Mike Y Chen. igrasp: grasp-based adaptive keyboard for mobile devices. In *Proceedings of the SIGCHI conference on human factors in computing systems*, pages 3037–3046. ACM, 2013.

[6] Connor Dickie, Roel Vertegaal, Changuk Sohn, and Daniel Cheng. eyelook: using attention to facilitate mobile media consumption. In *Proceedings of the 18th annual ACM symposium on User interface software and technology*, pages 103–106. ACM, 2005.

[7] Heiko Drewes, Alexander De Luca, and Albrecht Schmidt. Eye-gaze interaction for mobile phones. In *Proceedings of the 4th international conference on mobile technology, applications, and systems and the 1st international symposium on Computer human interaction in mobile technology*, pages 364–371. ACM, 2007.

[8] Augusto Esteves, Eduardo Velloso, Andreas Bulling, and Hans Gellersen. Orbits: Gaze interaction for smart watches using smooth pursuit eye movements. In *Proceedings of the 28th Annual ACM Symposium on User Interface Software & Technology*, pages 457–466. ACM, 2015.

[9] Ken Hinckley, Seongkook Heo, Michel Pahud, Christian Holz, Hrvoje Benko, Abigail Sellen, Richard Banks, Kenton O'Hara, Gavin Smyth, and William Buxton. Pre-touch sensing for mobile interaction. In *Proceedings of the 2016 CHI Conference on Human Factors in Computing Systems*, pages 2869–2881. ACM, 2016.

[10] Oliver Hohlfeld, André Pomp, Jó Ágila Bitsch Link, and Dennis Guse. On the applicability of computer vision based gaze tracking in mobile scenarios. In *Proceedings of the 17th International Conference on Human-Computer Interaction with Mobile Devices and Services*, pages 427–434. ACM, 2015.

[11] Anke Huckauf and Mario H Urbina. Gazing with peyes: towards a universal input for various applications. In *Proceedings of the 2008 symposium on Eye tracking research & applications*, pages 51–54. ACM, 2008.

[12] Robert JK Jacob. What you look at is what you get: eye movement-based interaction techniques. In *Proceedings of the SIGCHI conference on Human factors in computing systems*, pages 11–18. ACM, 1990.

[13] Mohamed Khamis, Florian Alt, and Andreas Bulling. The past, present, and future of gaze-enabled handheld mobile devices: survey and lessons learned. In *Proceedings of the 20th International Conference on Human-Computer Interaction with Mobile Devices and Services*, page 38. ACM, 2018.

[14] Mohamed Khamis, Mariam Hassib, Emanuel von Zezschwitz, Andreas Bulling, and Florian Alt. Gazetouchpin: protecting sensitive data on mobile devices using secure multimodal authentication. In *Proceedings of the 19th ACM International Conference on Multimodal Interaction*, pages 446–450. ACM, 2017.

[15] Jaewon Kim, Paul Thomas, Ramesh Sankaranarayana, Tom Gedeon, and Hwan-Jin Yoon. Eye-tracking analysis of user behavior and performance in web search on large and small screens. *Journal of the Association for Information Science and Technology*, 66(3):526–544, 2015.

[16] Manu Kumar, Tal Garfinkel, Dan Boneh, and Terry Winograd. Reducing shoulder-surfing by using gaze-based password entry. In *Proceedings of the 3rd symposium on Usable privacy and security*, pages 13–19. ACM, 2007.

[17] Andrew Kurauchi, Wenxin Feng, Ajjen Joshi, Carlos Morimoto, and Margrit Betke. Eye-swipe: Dwell-free text entry using gaze paths. In *Proceedings of the 2016 CHI Conference on Human Factors in Computing Systems*, pages 1952–1956. ACM, 2016.

[18] I Scott MacKenzie and R William Soukoreff. Phrase sets for evaluating text entry techniques. In *CHI'03 extended abstracts on Human factors in computing systems*, pages 754–755. ACM, 2003.

[19] Päivi Majaranta and Kari-Jouko Räihä. Twenty years of eye typing: systems and design issues. In *ETRA*, volume 2, pages 15–22, 2002.

[20] Alexander Mariakakis, Mayank Goel, Md Tanvir Islam Aumi, Shwetak N Patel, and Jacob O Wobbrock. Switchback: Using focus and saccade tracking to guide users' attention for mobile task resumption. In *Proceedings of the 33rd Annual ACM Conference on Human Factors in Computing Systems*, pages 2953–2962. ACM, 2015.

[21] Emiliano Miluzzo, Tianyu Wang, and Andrew T Campbell. Eyephone: activating mobile phones with your eyes. In *Proceedings of the second ACM SIGCOMM workshop on Networking, systems, and applications on mobile handhelds*, pages 15–20. ACM, 2010.

[22] Dan Odell and Vasudha Chandrasekaran. Enabling comfortable thumb interaction in tablet computers: a windows 8 case study. In *Proceedings of the Human Factors and Ergonomics Society Annual Meeting*, volume 56, pages 1907–1911. SAGE Publications Sage CA: Los Angeles, CA, 2012.

[23] Ken Pfeuffer, Jason Alexander, Ming Ki Chong, and Hans Gellersen. Gaze-touch: combining gaze with multi-touch for interaction on the same surface. In *Proceedings of the 27th annual ACM symposium on User interface software and technology*, pages 509–518. ACM, 2014.

[24] Ken Pfeuffer, Jason Alexander, Ming Ki Chong, Yanxia Zhang, and Hans Gellersen. Gaze-shifting: Direct-indirect input with pen and touch modulated by gaze. In *Proceedings of the 28th Annual ACM Symposium on User Interface Software & Technology*, pages 373–383. ACM, 2015.

[25] Ken Pfeuffer and Hans Gellersen. Gaze and touch interaction on tablets. In *Proceedings of the 29th Annual Symposium on User Interface Software and Technology*, pages 301–311. ACM, 2016.

[26] Ken Pfeuffer, Ken Hinckley, Michel Pahud, and Bill Buxton. Thumb+ pen interaction on tablets. In *CHI*, pages 3254–3266, 2017.

[27] Vijay Rajanna and John Paulin Hansen. Gaze typing in virtual reality: impact of keyboard design, selection method, and motion. In *Proceedings of the 2018 ACM Symposium on Eye Tracking Research & Applications*, page 15. ACM, 2018.

[28] Korok Sengupta, Raphael Menges, Chandan Kumar, and Steffen Staab. Gazethekey: Interactive keys to integrate word predictions for gaze-based text entry. In *Proceedings of the 22nd International Conference on Intelligent User Interfaces Companion*, pages 121–124. ACM, 2017.

[29] B. Shneiderman. Direct manipulation: A step beyond programming languages. *Computer*, 16(8):57–69, Aug 1983.

[30] Linda E Sibert and Robert JK Jacob. Evaluation of eye gaze interaction. In *Proceedings of the SIGCHI conference on Human Factors in Computing Systems*, pages 281–288. ACM, 2000.

[31] Sophie Stellmach and Raimund Dachselt. Look & touch: gaze-supported target acquisition. In *Proceedings of the SIGCHI Conference on Human Factors in Computing Systems*, pages 2981–2990. ACM, 2012.

[32] Tobii. Tobii 4c. https://gaming.tobii.com/product/tobii-eye-tracker-4c/, 2019.

[33] Tobii. Tobii eyex. https://gaming.tobii.com/products/peripherals/, 2019.

[34] Matthieu B Trudeau, Paul J Catalano, Devin L Jindrich, and Jack T Dennerlein. Tablet keyboard configuration affects performance, discomfort and task difficulty for thumb typing in a two-handed grip. *PloS one*, 8(6):e67525, 2013.

[35] Outi Tuisku, Päivi Majaranta, Poika Isokoski, and Kari-Jouko Räihä. Now dasher! dash away!: longitudinal study of fast text entry by eye gaze. In *Proceedings of the 2008 symposium on Eye tracking research & applications*, pages 19–26. ACM, 2008.

[36] Jayson Turner, Jason Alexander, Andreas Bulling, and Hans Gellersen. Gaze+ rst: integrating gaze and multitouch for remote rotate-scale-translate tasks. In *Proceedings of the 33rd Annual ACM Conference on Human Factors in Computing Systems*, pages 4179–4188. ACM, 2015.

[37] Jayson Turner, Andreas Bulling, Jason Alexander, and Hans Gellersen. Cross-device gaze-supported point-to-point content transfer. In *Proceedings of the Symposium on Eye Tracking Research and Applications*, pages 19–26. ACM, 2014.

[38] Jayson Turner, Andreas Bulling, and Hans Gellersen. Combining gaze with manual interaction to extend physical reach. In *Proceedings of the 1st international workshop on pervasive eye tracking & mobile eye-based interaction*, pages 33–36. ACM, 2011.

[39] Vytautas Vaitukaitis and Andreas Bulling. Eye gesture recognition on portable devices. In *Proceedings of the 2012 ACM Conference on Ubiquitous Computing*, pages 711–714. ACM, 2012.

[40] Julie Wagner, Stéphane Huot, and Wendy Mackay. Bitouch and bipad: designing bimanual interaction for hand-held tablets. In *Proceedings of the SIGCHI Conference on Human Factors in Computing Systems*, pages 2317–2326. ACM, 2012.

[41] David J Ward, Alan F Blackwell, and David JC MacKay. Dasher-a data entry interface using continuous gestures and language models. In *UIST*, pages 129–137. Citeseer, 2000.

[42] David J Ward and David JC MacKay. Artificial intelligence: fast hands-free writing by gaze direction. *Nature*, 418(6900):838, 2002.

[43] Katrin Wolf and Niels Henze. Comparing pointing techniques for grasping hands on tablets. In *Proceedings of the 16th international conference on Human-computer interaction with mobile devices & services*, pages 53–62. ACM, 2014.

[44] Katrin Wolf, Markus Schneider, John Mercouris, and Christopher-Eyk Hrabia. Biomechanics of front and back-of-tablet pointing with grasping hands. *International Journal of Mobile Human Computer Interaction (IJMHCI)*, 7(2):43–64, 2015.

[45] Erroll Wood and Andreas Bulling. Eyetab: Model-based gaze estimation on unmodified tablet computers. In *Proceedings of the Symposium on Eye Tracking Research and Applications*, pages 207–210. ACM, 2014.

[46] Shumin Zhai, Carlos Morimoto, and Steven Ihde. Manual and gaze input cascaded (magic) pointing. In *Proceedings of the SIGCHI conference on Human Factors in Computing Systems*, pages 246–253. ACM, 1999.